DENNIS DOHENY
Of Land and Sea

September 24 – October 22, 2011

Beverly Hills Location

Exclusive Representation by:

WILLIAM A. KARGES FINE ART

Carmel Gallery | 6th & Dolores, Carmel, California 93921 | 831.625.4266

Los Angeles Gallery | 427 N. Canon Drive #101, Beverly Hills, California 90210 | 310.276.8551

www.kargesfineart.com

32 x 38 inches   *Evening on the Santa Ynez*   Oil on Linen

Dennis Doheny, American Landscape Master

by Jean Stern – Museum Director

Dennis Doheny is one of the great American landscape painters of our time. Having been an art dealer, an art historian, a college-level art history instructor and a museum director specializing in American landscapes during my career, I have seen a great number of paintings. On my short list of the very best contemporary landscape artists, Dennis Doheny is at the top.

Curiously, it was in one of my previous incarnations, which is to say as an art dealer, that I met Dennis Doheny. From 1978 to 1991, I was director of Petersen Galleries, on Rodeo Drive in Beverly Hills. Petersen Galleries had a well-earned distinction for handling only the very best examples of California Impressionism, and we had never represented a living artist. One day in 1983, the gallery owner, Robert E. Petersen, chairman of the Petersen Publishing Company and founder of the Petersen Automotive Museum, came into the gallery with one of his close friends, Tim Doheny. To my utter disbelief, Petersen announced that the gallery would henceforth represent Doheny's son, Dennis. I had never heard of Dennis Doheny and I am certain that Petersen had never even seen a painting by Doheny's son, but that didn't matter, Petersen Galleries now represented Dennis Doheny.

Within a few days, Dennis came to the gallery and brought several of his paintings. To my relief, his paintings were very good and I was immediately converted. Here was a pleasant and polite young man who was much too young to paint as well as he did. His paintings were beautiful and strikingly executed with all the sureness of an experienced artist. To be sure, his paintings sold well and we continued to display his work until Petersen Galleries closed in 1991, when the Petersen Publishing Company was sold.

To be a great landscape painter, an artist has to truly love the land. Dennis shows that in every one of his pictures. His intimacy for the landscape compels him to be there in the very landscape he wants to paint. Dennis will paint a small oil sketch outdoors, then go back to the studio, use the small painting as his guide and paint the large, majestic final work.

The concept of painting outdoors is called "plein air" painting, an approach that Dennis has utilized throughout his career. The term plein-air comes from the French phrase en plein-air which is an idiom that does not translate directly, but simply means "outdoors."

Plein air painting is a specialized approach that landscape artists have practiced for over one hundred and fifty years. It is unquestionably the landscape painter's most effective tool, and like any tool, one needs to learn its proper uses as well as its limitations. When followed to its completion, the plein air technique has proven that it is the best approach to render natural light.

Natural light does not stand still, and more than any other artist, the landscape painter is mesmerized by its qualities. The passion for light drives them to seek the genuine experience and paint it, regardless of climate, weather or natural impediments. Hence, it is as a plein-air painter that the landscape artist finds his ultimate reason for being, and at the same time, confronts his most rigorous challenge: to capture quickly the brilliant and fluid visual sensation of natural light at a specific time and place while facing the formidable constraint of its fleeting characteristics.

The first painters credited with painting en plein-air in a systematic manner were the artists of the Barbizon School. Originally a small group of Parisian artists of the 1830s, they broke with French tradition by rejecting the pre-set conventions of the Academic manner. By 1848, the Barbizon painters had left Paris for the natural beauty of the Barbizon Forest, where they interacted with nature and recorded their experiences by painting en plein air.

At the same time, the tradition of American landscape painting had begun when a small group of dedicated painters gathered to record the beauty of nature. Now called the Hudson River School, artists such as Asher B. Durand (1796-1866), Sanford R. Gifford (1823-1880), Francis Silva (1835-1886), and George Inness (1825-1894) produced grand works of landscape, fully imbued with natural light.

On an international scale, it was the French Impressionists who, following upon the footsteps of the Barbizon painters, became the great popularizers of plein air painting. Impressionist landscapes were distinctive and drew both severe criticism and high praise for their convincing effect of true natural light. In time, Impressionism came to the United States, and by 1900, it became the style of choice among American painters.

The long and noble tradition of American landscape painting has continued to our own time and Dennis Doheny is an acknowledged master of the genre. To me, the most important aspect of a landscape painting is the light. Certainly, drawing, perspective and composition are important in any representational work of art, but for landscape, the light is the alpha and omega of it all. Dennis looks back on his artistic lineage, from the French Barbizon, to the Hudson River painters, and to the Impressionists. Intuitively, he consolidates aspects from each tradition and then adds his own modern approach to color handling. The result makes his paintings unique and unmistakable. To me, the most meritorious element in Dennis' work is his ability to convey natural light.

This is the first one man show that Dennis has had in five years. In that time, he has been busy painting and exhibiting throughout the country. In 2006, upon his first showing at the Prix de West Invitational Art Exhibition, held in Oklahoma City at the National Cowboy & Western Heritage Museum, Dennis won the Frederic Remington Award, a prize given in recognition of exceptional artistic merit in a painting. He won the Frederic Remington Award again, in 2008. In 2009, he received the Edgar Payne Gold Medal at the 98th Annual California Art Club Gold Medal Exhibition. It is only fitting that this award, named for Edgar Payne, the great landscape painter of the early 20th century, should be presented to Dennis Doheny, who many say is destined to be the seminal American landscape artist of the early 21st century.

In closing, we have come to the most interesting and rewarding point in this overview of what makes Dennis Doheny a master: viewing his art. All that's left is for we, the viewers, to immerse ourselves in the monumental beauty of his paintings.

Plates

Reflections of Dawn

Center: 12 x 16 inches

Outer panels: 12 x 9 inches

Oil on Linen

September's Warmth

24 x 30 inches

Oil on Linen

Phosphorescent Sea

20 x 24 inches

Oil on Linen

Sycamore and Lupine

20 x 24 inches

Oil on Linen

Moonlight from the Rim

36 x 40 inches

Oil on Linen

Sunrise – Owens Valley

24 x 30 inches

Oil on Linen

Torrey Pines

24 x 30 inches

Oil on Linen

Fall Aspens

16 x 20 inches

Oil on Linen

Emerald Coast

11 x 14 inches

Oil on Linen

Gato Canyon Poppies

20 x 24 inches

Oil on Linen

Slipping into Evening

24 x 30 inches

Oil on Linen

Lamp Lit Dawn

16 x 20 inches

Oil on Linen

Morning Palms

40 x 40 inches

Oil on Linen

Autumn Sycamores

36 x 46 inches

Oil on Linen

Scripps Park – La Jolla

16 x 20 inches

Oil on Linen

Arrival of Spring

24 x 30 inches

Oil on Linen

Exhibition History

Solo Exhibitions

1997 "Visions of California", William A. Karges Fine Art
1999 "Recent Work", William A. Karges Fine Art
2000 "New Paintings", William A. Karges Fine Art
2001 "Recent Work", William A. Karges Fine Art
2003 "A Sense of Place", William A. Karges Fine Art
2005 "Celebrating California", William A. Karges Fine Art
2006 "Light on the Land", William A. Karges Fine Art
2011 "Of Land and Sea", William A. Karges Fine Art

Group Exhibitions

1998 "Treasures of the Sierra Nevada", California Art Club, Los Angeles Natural History Museum and Muckenthaler Cultural Center

Carmel Art Festival, Carmel, CA

88th Gold Medal Exhibition, California Art Club, Pasadena Historical Museum

2000 Spring Salon, California Art Club, Edenhurst and Morseburg Galleries, Los Angeles

89th Gold Medal Exhibition, California Art Club, Pasadena Historical Museum

2001 90th Gold Medal Exhibition, California Art Club, Pasadena Historical Museum

California Art Club Painting Festival, San Juan Capistrano

Spring Salon, California Art Club, Edenhurst and Morseburg Galleries, Los Angeles

2002 Masters of the American West, Autry National Center, Los Angeles

Scape, Santa Barbara, CA
Four Contemporary Artists, The California Club, Los Angeles

91st Gold Medal Exhibition, California Art Club, Pasadena Historical Museum

Valley Club Western Art Exhibition, Montecito, CA

Western Visions, National Museum of Wildlife Art, Jackson, WY

2003 Masters of the American West, Autry National Center, Los Angeles

On Location in Malibu, Frederick R. Weisman Museum of Art, Pepperdine University, Malibu, CA

Western Visions, National Museum of Wildlife Art, Jackson, WY

92nd Gold Medal Exhibition, California Art Club, Pasadena Museum of California Art

2004 Masters of the American West, Autry National Center, Los Angeles

Western Visions, National Museum of Wildlife Art, Jackson, WY

93rd Gold Medal Exhibition, California Art Club, Pasadena Museum of California Art

2005 Masters of the American West, Autry National Center, Los Angeles

94th Gold Medal Exhibition, California Art Club, Pasadena Museum of California Art

2006 Masters of the American West, Autry National Center, Los Angeles, CA

95th Gold Medal Exhibition, California Art Club, Pasadena Museum of California Art

"Malibu", Frederick R. Weisman Museum of Art, Pepperdine University, Malibu, CA

Prix de West Invitational Art Exhibition, National Cowboy and Western Heritage Museum, Oklahoma City, OK

"Quest for the West", Eiteljorg Museum of American Indians and Western Art, Indianapolis, IN

Western Visions, National Museum of Wildlife Art, Jackson, WY

2007 Masters of the American West, Autry National Center, Los Angeles, CA

96th Gold Medal Exhibition, California Art Club, Pasadena Museum of California Art

Prix de West Invitational Art Exhibition, National Cowboy and Western Heritage Museum, Oklahoma City, OK

"Quest for the West", Eiteljorg Museum of American Indians and Western Art, Indianapolis, IN

Western Visions, National Museum of Wildlife Art, Jackson, WY

2008 Masters of the American West, Autry National Center, Los Angeles, CA

97th Gold Medal Exhibition, California Art Club, Pasadena Museum of California Art

Prix de West Invitational Art Exhibition, National Cowboy and Western Heritage Museum, Oklahoma City, OK

"Quest for the West", Eiteljorg Museum of American Indians and Western Art, Indianapolis, IN

Western Visions, National Museum of Wildlife Art, Jackson, WY

American Masters, Salmagundi Club, New York, NY

2009 Masters of the American West, Autry National Center, Los Angeles, CA

98th Gold Medal Exhibition, California Art Club, Pasadena Museum of California Art

Prix de West Invitational Art Exhibition, National Cowboy and Western Heritage Museum, Oklahoma City, OK

"Quest for the West", Eiteljorg Museum of American Indians and Western Art, Indianapolis, IN

Western Visions, National Museum of Wildlife Art, Jackson, WY

American Masters, Salmagundi Club, New York, NY

2010 Masters of the American West, Autry National Center, Los Angeles, CA

99th Gold Medal Exhibition, California Art Club, Pasadena Museum of California Art

Prix de West Invitational Art Exhibition, National Cowboy and Western Heritage Museum, Oklahoma City, OK

Glenna Hartmann Invitational Fine Art Exhibition, Santa Barbara Natural History Museum, Santa Barbara, CA

Western Visions, National Museum of Wildlife Art, Jackson, WY

American Masters, Salmagundi Club, New York, NY

Los Angeles Country Club Invitational Paint-Out, Los Angeles, CA

2011 Masters of the American West, Autry National Center, Los Angeles, CA

100th Gold Medal Exhibition, California Art Club, Pasadena Museum of California Art

Prix de West Invitational Art Exhibition, National Cowboy and Western Heritage Museum, Oklahoma City, OK

American Masters, Salmagundi Club, New York, NY

Awards	1999	Gold Medal, Carmel Art Festival
		Honorable Mention, 89th Gold Medal Exhibition, California Art Club
	2000	Inaugural Granville Redmond Purchase Prize, Spring Salon, California Art Club
	2001	Blue Ribbon Award, Scape, Santa Barbara, CA
	2003	Masters of the American West Award, Purchase Prize, Autry National Center
	2006	Frederic Remington Award, Prix de West Invitational Art Exhibition
		Quest for the West Purchase Prize, Eiteljorg Museum
	2008	Frederic Remington Award, Prix de West Invitational Art Exhibition
	2009	Edgar Payne Award, 99th Gold Medal Exhibition, California Art Club
		Masters of the American West Bohlin Buckle, Outstanding Artistic Achievement, Autry National Center

Selected Publications

February 1999, American Artist Magazine
May 1999, "Artists to Watch", Southwest Art
April/May 2000, "Spotlight", Art-Talk
January/February 2001, "Emotional Connections", Art of the West
May 2003, "California Painters", Southwest Art
June 2003, "Coming of Age", Art & Antiques
May/June 2004, "For the Love of the Land", Art of the West,
May 2005, "Dennis Doheny: Painting the Land that He Loves", Plein Air Magazine
November 2005, "The Studio", Art of the West
Summer 2006, "Painting the Great Outdoors", California Art Club Newsletter
Summer 2006, "Doheny Wins Remington Honor", Persimmon Hill Magazine
May 2008, "A Love Affair with Life", Prix de West Preview
November 2008, "Striving for Atmosphere and Detail", American Artist Magazine
June 2009, "Trail Talk", Montecito Journal
Summer 2009, "A Simple Garage Makeover", American Artist Magazine
January/February 2010, 'Light is the Key", Art of the West
June 2010, "Cream of the Crop", Southwest Art
August 2010, "Free Spirit", Western Art Collector
2011, California Light: A Century of Landscapes, published by Skira Rizzoli